Original title:
The Living Room of Love

Copyright © 2025 Creative Arts Management OÜ
All rights reserved.

Author: Miriam Kensington
ISBN HARDBACK: 978-1-80587-139-2
ISBN PAPERBACK: 978-1-80587-609-0

Ribbons of Radiance

In corners, a cat lazily sprawls,
While cushions catch jokes, where laughter calls.
A dance of socks on the wooden floor,
As mismatched pairs plot to start a war.

The coffee table wears crumbs like a crown,
While an old sitcom plays, and the cat frowns.
Spilled soda on the carpet, bright and wild,
Mom's plant thinks it's been adopted by a child.

Grandma's stories float like balloons in air,
Filling the space with moments to share.
The walls are painted with memories spry,
As ghosts of the past wink and jog by.

The remote's a treasure, lost on a quest,
While pillows conspire to offer their best.
In this joyful chaos, we find pure delight,
In ribbons of radiance, laughter takes flight.

Sunrise in the Room

Sunlight dances through curtains of gold,
Tickling the sleepy, the young and the old.
A cereal box sings in an off-key tune,
As we gather the spoons to join the cartoon.

Mismatched mugs brew stories we sip,
While socks play hide and seek in a quip.
The clock on the wall ticks in laughter's sway,
Counting giggles as the morning slips away.

The dog plays the piano with paws full of glee,
While kids perform concerts for all to see.
A parade of the oddities lines the couch,
As we cheer for the moments that make us crouch.

Snuggled together, we laugh till we ache,
In this wild sunlit room, we dance and partake.
With joyful chaos painting our hearts so bright,
Each sunrise declares our love in pure light.

Chasing Dreams on Soft Cushions

On the couch we nap and dream,
With popcorn crumbs our only theme.
The cat thinks it's a throne, not shared,
As we giggle at the mess we dared.

With blankets tossed like fashion trends,
And pillows arguing with us, friends.
We chase the snacks that roll away,
In this cushion kingdom, we laugh and play.

Sanctuary of Togetherness

Socks mismatched, a sight to see,
A fortress built of harmony.
With ice cream fights and tickle wars,
Life's too short, let's not keep scores.

We share our dreams, our wildest quips,
With chocolate stains on endless lips.
In this cozy nook, we bloom and sway,
A ruckus love, come what may.

The Palette of Affection

Colors splashed on walls we own,
A canvas bright that we've outgrown.
With laughter as our finest hue,
And every joke a stroke anew.

Splatters of joy around the room,
With messy hearts that brightly bloom.
Each funny mishap a work of art,
In this silly gallery, we won't part.

Flickering Flames of Connection

The candle flickers, shadows dance,
We fumble, giggle, caught in trance.
With every laugh, a warmth we feel,
Conclusion's clear, it's quite the deal.

Hot cocoa spills, but who would frown?
We sip our drinks, then splash it down!
With banter bright, the evening's gone,
Our fondness glows, a lively dawn.

Comfort in Every Corner

Pillow forts and tangled socks,
Laughter echoes, time unlocks.
A cat who thinks she's queen for a day,
Snoozing while we laugh and play.

Chips and dips spill on the floor,
We chase the crumbs, always wanting more.
In this chaos, love's the key,
To our home filled with glee.

The Glow of Shared Moments

Couch cushions turn into a stage,
As we perform, uncaged and brave.
A spotlight made of kitchen light,
Dancing shadows in the night.

Mismatched socks are now the norm,
In this cozy, cluttered form.
Laughter's aroma fills the air,
A fragrance of joy beyond compare.

Emblems of Affection

Fridge magnets holding hearts in place,
Every silly note, a warm embrace.
Sticky fingers from ice cream treats,
A symphony of messy feats.

Cupcakes with candles, a frost on my nose,
Silly fights where the giggle grows.
Each face forgotten, blurred like a dream,
Caught in the moment, an endless beam.

Together in the Twilight

TV shows with nonsense plots,
We're laughing hard, forgetting thoughts.
Pajama parties for just two,
In this haven, love feels brand new.

Night falls, we swap our tales,
With popcorn wars, we never fail.
A life adorned with glittering quirks,
Here's where joy and comfort works.

The Soundtrack of Heartstrings

The radio plays our silly tunes,
While we dance like clumsy buffoons.
Pillows become our trusted stage,
As we laugh and unleash our rage.

Each laugh echoes, a sweet silly chime,
Mixed with giggles, it feels like prime time.
Remotes fly like frisbees, oh what a sight,
Love's soundtrack plays on, from morning 'til night.

Whispers on the Sofa

Whispers float on a cushiony throne,
Secret tales to a soft fabric tone.
Gossip arrives with a popcorn crunch,
As we snuggle in for a cozy brunch.

The cat joins in with a sassy meow,
Claiming her spot, she's queen of the wow.
We giggle and tease, trading old jokes,
As the afternoon blooms in fits of hoaxes.

Heartbeats in the Cozy Nook

In a corner where cushions collide,
We chat about dreams with laughter as our guide.
The clock ticks slow, under blankets we hide,
Like two little kids on a joy-fueled ride.

Our snacks are shared with delight and with cheer,
Oops! A chocolate spills, oh dear, oh dear!
Yet with each sweet mess and every small sigh,
Our hearts beat a rhythm, as time passes by.

Embrace of the Evening Glow

Under soft lights where shadows play,
We spin silly tales, come what may.
Each punchline dances under starlit skies,
As we trip through stories, laughter never dies.

Blankets wrapped tight like a cozy embrace,
Every moment shared, a warm-hearted race.
With each silly mishap and twinkling eyes,
The glow of love's laughter forever complies.

Tales Told by Firelight

The flames crackle, tell a tale,
Of socks mismatched, dogs that wail.
Grandpa's stories, all in jest,
Of epic fails we loved the best.

Marshmallows roast, they melt away,
In gooey laughter, we will stay.
The shadows leap, they make us grin,
As memories twirl, where laughter's been.

Where Shadows Dance

Shadows twist like silly dreams,
Behind the couch, they burst at seams.
A cat on the shelf, looking quite posh,
Claims every seat with a royal swash.

We dance on cushions, soft and bright,
While snacks go missing in the night.
With hiccupping giggles, we share a chair,
Who knew mere furniture could ever care?

Comfort in the Corners

In corners shall we find delight,
Where pillows chat and blanket fights.
The lost remotes, they hide and seek,
In laughter's warmth, we hear them squeak.

A couch that groans, but holds our tales,
As friendship's ship sails through the gales.
With popcorn clouds, we float and soar,
In this cozy spot, we always want more.

Mosaics of Togetherness

Bits of laughter like shattered glass,
Creating beauty in moments that pass.
Board games sprawled like art anew,
As rules are bent and chaos grew.

With socks on hands, we make our show,
And steal the scenes, a time to glow.
In this mosaic, each piece shines bright,
In love and laughter, we take flight.

Warmth Beneath the Rug

A cat stretched out on a sunny spot,
While underneath, we hide the hot chocolate pot.
The dog snores loudly, it's a cozy scene,
With marshmallow dreams wrapped in blue and green.

The couch collects crumbs with a loving frown,
As laughter echoes, not a trace of a frown.
We trip over toys, and yet we grin,
In this playful chaos, all is tucked in.

Laughter in Every Corner

There's a sock on the lamp, what a sight to behold,
The story of messiness never gets old.
Pillows are thrown in a playful duel,
And giggles rain down like a fanciful rule.

The clock ticks slowly, but time flies like air,
As we share secret snacks with a mischievous flair.
Remote controls vanish, it's part of the game,
In this house of joy, we're all quite the same.

The Art of Shared Silence

In quiet moments, we glance and we smirk,
Our eyes trade secrets, while no one will jerk.
An unspoken bond, like a cozy embrace,
With popcorn and pillows, we each find our place.

The TV's a background, our laughter is loud,
As silent chuckles link us, we feel quite proud.
A shared smile ignites when the cat makes a dive,
In the stillness, we find that we're so very alive.

Glances Across the Sofa

A wink from across, oh what could it mean?
Peeking through cushions, a sly little scene.
We plot our next snack like a heist on the run,
A giggle erupts; oh, isn't this fun?

The blanket fort's built, an ambitious delight,
While shadows dance wildly, we're safe from the night.
With game controllers poised, let the fun never end,
In our quirky little kingdom, we're all the best friends.

Shelves Full of Dreams

Dusty books that laugh at me,
Their spines cracked, but oh so free.
A cat naps on the open page,
Plot twists on a feline stage.

Coffee stains, a memory guide,
Whispers of adventures wide.
Imaginations run amok,
Shelf life that can't be stuck.

Fragrant Moments

Candles flicker, scents collide,
Cinnamon and chaos side by side.
Popcorn kernels dance in air,
Sticky notes with love laid bare.

Laughter spilled like spilled red wine,
A mix of giggles, oh so fine.
Socks that vanish, where'd they go?
In this space, the quirks will flow.

Serenity Under the Chandelier

That chandelier sways with flair,
While mismatched chairs take up the air.
A game of charades in plain sight,
With laundry lurking, what a sight!

Puzzle pieces scatter about,
Voices echo, laugh and shout.
With every snack, a story glows,
Under the lights, hilarity flows.

Reflections of Us

Mirrors show us silly grins,
Dance moves that are sure to spin.
A couch that creaks with every leap,
In this space, we find our keep.

Fluffy blankets, pillow fights,
Just the place for fairy lights.
Moments captured, quirky and bright,
We're shining stars all through the night.

Memories in Multicolors

Bright cushions scatter round the floor,
Tangled stories, we can't ignore.
Milk spilled on the brand new rug,
Laughter echoes; we hug and shrug.

Pastel stains on old white walls,
A thousand giggles in the halls.
Oven burnt, a culinary flop,
Yet slapstick tales just never stop.

Unraveled in Relaxation

Socks mismatched in a lazy heap,
TV blaring, the couchbirds sleep.
A snack attack in sofa's depth,
Every cranny holds a hidden theft.

Remote control is lost once more,
Under cushions, ten times four.
We dive in; what a silly mess,
Love's a game, but who's the best?

Gentle Conversations

Whispers float like bubbles bright,
Each word dressed in pure delight.
Silly secrets, chuckled fate,
Time pauses just to contemplate.

Mispronounced words turn into glee,
Like rapping cats or dancing trees.
We share the mundane, clothed in fun,
In endless chats, we're never done.

The Silence Between Us

Quiet moments, tic-tac clock,
Legs tangled up, beneath the sock.
A glance exchanged, like playful jest,
In stillness, we find our shared quest.

Who's snoring louder? A riveting game,
Paper crinkles, igniting our flame.
The silence hums with our quirky beats,
As love thrives in our funny seats.

Cradled in Warmth

In cozy corners, laughter dwells,
With mismatched socks and funny smells.
A cat who thinks he's king of the chair,
Snoozes deeply without a care.

Half-eaten snacks on the table abound,
As we bounce on cushions, giggles surround.
Popcorn fights and game night debates,
We settle disputes with chocolate plates.

The TV's on but hardly tuned in,
We're serving up chaos with a cheeky grin.
Every story shared turns into a roast,
We treasure these moments, they matter the most.

Clarity in Candlelight

With flickering flames illuminating the scene,
We pretend we're adults, so classy, so keen.
Yet someone spills juice, and all is a mess,
We laugh it off, oh, what a guess!

A game of charades with an old shoe in hand,
Each silent gesture is hilariously grand.
Candles wobble, and shadows dance free,
As we dive into stories, just you and me.

Pizza delivery? Oh, that's a delight!
Cheesy hangouts that last through the night.
Candlelight flickers on smiles so bright,
Creating a joy that feels just right.

Echoes of Laughter

Echoes of laughter bounce off the walls,
As friends spill secrets and tumble like balls.
We play silly games, and our laughter abounds,
With playful remarks, we're all laughter-bound.

An old recliner, its springs a bit shy,
Cracks and complains as we waddle by.
Cushions become forts in our little retreat,
In this maze of laughter, we're hardly discreet.

We swap wild tales that get wilder with time,
Each story enriched, like a well-crafted rhyme.
As night drifts on, and we roll on the floor,
We find all our worries, we just can't ignore.

Secrets Between Cushions

Between the cushions, where secrets lie,
Are whispered tales and a little sly cry.
A missing remote, a snack stash so rare,
We dig through the fluff, our treasure to share.

The sofa is sagging, it knows all our quirks,
As we leak our dreams with a giggle that jerks.
Hidden sweet notes under cushions we find,
Each one a clue in this life so intertwined.

Jokes float around like dust in the air,
Every noticeable look met with laughter and flair.
In this cozy spot, with moments so grand,
Friends unite, holding hands in this land.

Hearth of Whispered Secrets

On a couch of faded plaid,
We spill our hearts like tea,
Laughter floats like popcorn,
In this cozy sanctuary.

The cat knocks over a lamp,
Our cheers turn into roars,
The remote plays hide and seek,
As we tumble on the floors.

Mismatched socks dance on the rug,
A fortress made of pillows,
We wage a battle of tickles,
While the clock just watches, still.

The walls are filled with our jokes,
Echoes of laughter cling,
In a space where love is loud,
And silliness is the king.

Cozy Embrace of Shadows

Under blankets, secrets hide,
Food fights break, oh what fun,
Cushions fly like soft grenades,
As we blush at things we've done.

The shadow puppets in the night,
Bring giggles in the dark,
With silly faces made of light,
We paint each other's spark.

The fridge hums a ballad sweet,
Leftovers in a bold romance,
Popcorn whispers in our ears,
While we swirl and spin in dance.

In corners, echoes of funny tales,
As laughter fills the air,
Love is messy, joy unveiled,
In this whimsical affair.

Where Hearts Nest

A fortress built of scattered books,
We dive into worlds anew,
Where the cat's our royal guard,
And the snacks just multiply too.

We play charades with goofy grins,
Accents and dances intertwine,
Our laughter's like an open door,
To a place that's truly divine.

The old clock ticks with smirking glee,
As each clue gets a wild guess,
Moments wrapped in laughter's arms,
In a state of pure success.

With every shared silly look,
The sun begins to set,
In this nest of joy and love,
The best place we can get.

Echoes of Togetherness

In the nook of mismatched chairs,
We're the riddle and the rhyme,
Sipping tea with silly straws,
Creating joy, one cup at a time.

The TV's noise, a friendly hum,
As we quiz each other's taste,
A chocolate bar becomes a prize,
In our hide-and-seek with haste.

With every tickle, wink, and sigh,
The cushions bloom with cheer,
We build our dreams on coffee cups,
Floating blissful through the year.

Laughter echoes in the walls,
A tune that won't forget,
In this patchwork of our hearts,
Together, we are set.

The Comfort of Familiarity

In corners where we laugh and play,
A worn-out couch holds sway today.
With cushions tossed and drinks a-fly,
We crack up, giggles reaching high.

The rug beneath is stained with cheer,
Last week's snacks are still quite near.
Old board games piled, a sight so grand,
With rules we twist, we take a stand.

Pictures frame our crazy crew,
A moment caught, a crazy view.
Silly faces, timeless hints,
Love's laughter echoes in these prints.

My Favorite Chair's Embrace

My chair reclines, it knows my name,
Each creak and crack, a cozy claim.
With popcorn bowl held high in reach,
It hears my dreams while I just breach.

It's where I plot my world renown,
With fuzzy socks and homemade crown.
My throne of comfort, soft and wide,
In its embrace, I love to hide.

Binge-watching tales, my heart's delight,
As neighbors peek from left and right.
My trusty chair, oh loyal mate,
With you, my life's a fun estate.

Nestled in Nostalgia

In corners where the warm light beams,
We share our quirkiest of dreams.
Old photos sprawl, with countless tales,
Of epic fails and funny gales.

The scent of cookies fills the air,
While socks fight for a comfy pair.
We reminisce, our hearts on fire,
With laughter, we build new desires.

Old toys lie thrown across the floor,
Each silent witness to our lore.
This space, a blend of joy and jest,
In cozy chaos, we feel blessed.

The Palette of Together

We splatter our days with vibrant hues,
Each quip and tease, each silly ruse.
With colors bold, we paint away,
In strokes of laughter, night or day.

Coffee spills and cookie crumbs,
Life's masterpiece of happy hums.
We swap tall tales, we paint the skies,
With smirks and nods, we improvise.

A dash of chaos, a sprinkle of fun,
Crafting memories, one by one.
In this bright corner, hearts entwine,
A canvas filled with love, divine.

Where Time Slows

In this space, the clock takes naps,
The cat joins in with playful flaps.
A cushion war, we laugh and dive,
In this cozy nook, we feel alive.

Remote's lost, but who needs TV?
We craft our stories, wild and free.
In laughter's sway, we lose all count,
Time's a joker, climbing the mount.

Chairs become thrones of silly glee,
With popcorn castles, we reign with glee.
The world outside can wait or dance,
In here we give the fun a chance.

Days fly by on fluffy clouds,
We wear our smiles like vibrant shrouds.
In this cozy haven, joy just grows,
In the magic of moments, time slows.

The Chair That Holds Us

That chair, a kingdom of snacks and dreams,
Where laughter bubbles and friendship beams.
Its cushions cradle our quirkiest chats,
A throne for mischief, and bouncy cats.

We share our secrets, both silly and bold.
With tales so wild, they never get old.
A battle for space, a gentle shove,
In our little kingdom, it's all pure love.

Its armrests bear the weight of our glee,
While cushions hide crumbs, a nightly spree.
Who knew a chair could hold so much cheer?
In its warm arms, we've no room for fear.

Together we lounge in hues of delight,
Crafting our lives in the soft twilight.
In the chair that holds us, we find our spark,
Turning mundane hours into joyful art.

Whispers of Yesterday

In the corners where memories stay,
Echoes of laughter dance and play.
Old tunes drag us into the past,
In these whispers, friendships last.

We recall the time when snacks went rogue,
And tackled the dog like a playful fog.
A spill of soda, a cloud of cheer,
In these tales, we find we're near.

Grandma's yarn, a tangled mess,
Turned into crowns; oh, what a dress!
Past moments swirl in a funny haze,
Turning the ordinary into a blaze.

Time may rush on with critical haste,
But in our hearts, it's never misplaced.
With every chuckle, each shared delight,
Yesterday's whispers light up the night.

Pastel Dreams

In hues of peach, we plan and scheme,
Where life feels like a funny dream.
With candy clouds and marshmallow skies,
We chase our laughter, oh how it flies!

Paint-splotched walls tell tales of fun,
Riddles unraveled, all in good pun.
A dance with socks and mismatched shoes,
In pastel schemes, we simply can't lose.

Cupcakes whisper sweet, silly things,
While our hearts rise and float on wings.
We toss confetti as moments bloom,
In a world that sparkles, banishing gloom.

So here we stay, with giggles that gleam,
Sipping life slowly, one tasty cream.
In pastel dreams, every laugh's our toast,
In this quirky color, we love the most.

Heartbeats in Harmony

In our cozy nest, we gather close,
Where laughter crackles, we boast and toast.
Tickles and giggles fill the air,
In a symphony played without a care.

Jokes about socks that don't seem to pair,
And bickering over who takes the chair.
With every heartbeat, a punchline flies,
While the dog rolls his eyes and sighs.

Remote control wars and snack attacks,
Fight over the last slice; no turning backs.
Yet we all find solace under this roof,
As each witty jab reveals the truth.

So here's to the madness, the fun, the cheers,
In a room where we share our hopes and fears.
With every laugh and every glance,
This joyful narra-tale continues to dance.

Pillows of Kindred Spirits

Cushions piled high, a soft fortress grand,
We battle for space, not by grand plan.
Throw pillows fly in a friendly squall,
Each pillow fight leads to laughter for all.

Mismatched socks and silly hairdos,
Trading old stories, sharing old news.
In this chaotic quilt of love, we find,
That laughter does bind, no bounds unlined.

There's a secret stash under the couch,
Of old candy wrappers and crumbs, we crouch.
As we munch on the spoils, secrets unfold,
In this kingdom of warmth, we never grow old.

A nest of blankets, a cozy embrace,
With a dash of chaos, we find our grace.
Kindred spirits unite in this tale,
And on laughter's breeze, we set our sail.

Reflections on the Coffee Table

The coffee stains tell a story, you see,
Of vibrant debates over who brewed the tea.
Mugs line up like soldiers in a row,
With tales of trips to the fridge in slow-mo.

A pile of magazines, scattered and tossed,
With the latest reality shows we've lost.
In this clutter, a treasure trove gleams,
Where our dreams pile high like forgotten themes.

Candles flicker while we tear up with glee,
At tales of mishaps on our daily spree.
Reflections of friendships dance in the light,
As we sip our brew and banter till night.

So raise a toast to the clutter, the fun,
For it's the simple moments that truly run.
On this table of life, we laugh and we cry,
In the tapestry woven, here's to you and I.

Shelves of Laughter and Tears

On these shelves sit memories, laughter's delight,
With photos of mishaps and moments so bright.
Each frame tells a tale of the silly and sweet,
Where joy walks with tears in a whimsical beat.

Dusty old trophies of games lost and won.
Competing for glory, all just for fun.
Here stands the evidence of pies that went wrong,
Yet everyone chuckles, singing the song.

Trinkets from travels stained with the years,
Reservoirs of joy mixed with splashes of tears.
With every quirky statue that sits in its spot,
We find a treasure in laughter, a lot!

So let's celebrate moments, the good and the mad,
In this rich tapestry, nothing's too bad.
With shelves of our laughter, we'll dance through this life,

In the glow of togetherness, free from strife.

Framed Dreams on the Walls

Above the couch, a picture hangs,
Of cats in hats, oh how it clangs.
They leap and dance on painted frames,
Who knew our laughter had such names?

A trophy from a toilet race,
At least we won, there's no disgrace.
With every trip, a quirk we find,
Our walls shout joy, and never mind!

The coffee mugs tell stories bold,
Of friendships forged in warmth and gold.
Each sip a giggle, sweet and bright,
Together we twirl into the night.

When guests arrive, we strike a pose,
In our dreamscape where silliness flows.
With each new frame, our tales unfold,
In this wild space, our hearts are sold.

The Scent of Time Well Spent

Cinnamon swirls in the air tonight,
As laughter bounces, a pure delight.
We share our snacks and endless whims,
Each story told, our joy begins.

With popcorn trails on our old rug,
We dance around, a silly thug.
The remote is lost in cozy folds,
Yet all feel rich, as life unfolds.

We wear our pajamas like a crown,
And spin in circles, never a frown.
The clock might tick, but who's to care?
In this soft chaos, love's our dare.

So raise your mug, let's toast this glee,
To minutes cherished, just you and me.
With every sip, the warmth returns,
In sweet, absurdity, our spirit burns.

Collecting Moments under the Ceiling

Beneath this dome of quirky dreams,
We gather giggles, and silly themes.
Each cushion fort a fortress grand,
With snack invasions from our hand.

The ceiling fan spins tales so wild,
Of silly faces, and laughter's child.
We catch the echoes of our glee,
In this fun space, just you and me.

With every glance, a moment's made,
In zany poses, we giggle displayed.
Our scrapbook grows with hearts that race,
Through clouded minds, we find our place.

So come join in, let's toss our cares,
On this ceiling, our joy declares.
With each adventure, we leap and leap,
Collecting moments, our heartbeats keep.

Light Filtering Through Love's Curtains

Sunlight dapples in playful streams,
Waking up laughter from our dreams.
The curtains flutter, dance, and sway,
Inviting joy to seize the day.

We play hide-and-seek with every ray,
Where shadows giggle, come out to play.
Each corner holds a friendly tease,
As whispers echo through the breeze.

With every flicker, fun ignites,
In light's embrace, our heart takes flight.
We chase the beams, a merry race,
In this bright space, our favorite place.

So open wide, let warmth come in,
With silly grins, let the fun begin.
Together we shine like stars above,
In this warm glimmer, we find love.

Paintings of Passion

On the wall, a cat hung low,
With a bowtie and a stylish flow.
He eyed the snacks, his crafty aim,
Cuz every nibble's part of the game.

Mom's portrait winks, the dad's in shock,
As the dog performs a silly rock.
Kids giggle loud, what a playful din,
In this gallery, we're all akin.

Coffee stains like masterpieces swirled,
A canvas of chaos, laughter unfurled.
The flowers are plastic, but who even cares?
In this space, love paints and laughter dares.

The couch is a ship, let's sail for a treat,
Navigating pillows, we're in for a feat.
With laughter as bright as the sun's morning rays,
This is our gallery—the best of all days.

Sheltered Connections

Under the blankets, we build a fort,
A kingdom of giggles, and no need for court.
Pillows as guards, they keep us so safe,
While snacks are our treasure; we're on a brave waif.

Mismatched socks are the fashion tonight.
As we debate whether the moon is a fright.
Hot chocolate spills, creating a mess,
But love's in the laughter, I must confess.

Lost in the maze of stories we share,
With movie marathons and popcorn to spare.
Each joke a thread in our quilt of delight,
We celebrate life in the softest of light.

The pets join the fun, losing all sense,
In this cozy retreat, there's no pretense.
So raise a toast with our cups held up high.
In this haven of joy, let the worries fly.

Cadence of Companionship

In this quirky nook where we all collide,
Dance parties erupt with no reason to hide.
Feathers and pillows afloat in the air,
As we boogie to tunes, without a care.

The cat meows loudly, he's joining the fun,
A furry DJ spinning tunes on the run.
With awkward shuffles, and humorous flair,
We paint every moment, a colorful share.

The clock ticks slowly—who needs to hurry?
Time stands still in this laughter-fueled flurry.
Jokes wrapped in giggles swirl 'round the space,
In this funky rhythm, we find our own pace.

So grab your dance shoes, let's leap and rejoice,
Each laugh helps us grow; it's our shared voice.
Together we find our own special beat,
In this vibrant cadence, our lives feel complete.

Threads of Light

With blanket forts spun from dreams overhead,
We craft our own world where the wild things tread.
Flashlights become magic, illuminating tales,
Of dragons and heroes, of ships with big sails.

That corner's our stage, where each laugh takes flight,
While socks play the chorus, a whimsical sight.
Mismatched and loud, they dance on the floor,
In this playful room, we always want more.

The coffee pot bubbles, spilling stories bright,
A calendar filled with each silly night.
We braid our adventures with threads loud and sweet,
Creating a fabric that feels like a treat.

In this haven of joy, where time drifts away,
We stitch every moment, come join in the play.
With laughter as glue, we bubble with cheer,
In these threads of light, our hearts are sincere.

Tapestry of Everyday Joy

A couch that swallows all our dreams,
With cushions flying like silly schemes.
The cat claims all the sunny spots,
While we debate on dinner pots.

The TV glows with laugh tracks loud,
As we tumble in our joyful crowd.
Popcorn fights and remote wars,
Turns our space into fun galore.

A dance-off breaks out with no tune,
Swirling to the sound of the afternoon.
Every tickle ignites a cheer,
In this place, we shed all fear.

With mugs of tea and stories tall,
We jest and giggle, let laughter call.
In this tapestry, our hearts weave tight,
A funny patchwork, pure delight.

Radiance of Familiar Touch

The blanket's frayed edge tells its tale,
How many times we've started to wail.
It's been our fortress through storms and gales,
Where silly secrets slip like snail trails.

A foot rub turns into a wrestling match,
Voices raise in a hilarious scratch.
Elastic farts echo off the walls,
As laughter bounces, it surely enthralls.

Mismatched socks drape like fallen leaves,
In this riot of comfort, no one believes.
We snicker at each other's coffee stains,
Cherishing our friendship like precious chairs.

This space a canvas, vibrant and bright,
Where even failures are sheer delight.
Through jests and jibes, we'll always thrive,
In this glow, our hearts feel alive.

Serenity in the Space Between

A quiet pause in the noisy whirl,
Laughter stirs like a playful twirl.
The coffee's brewing, a scent divine,
As we trade smirks over the old wine.

In the corners, memories twinkle and dance,
Each picture whispers of our crazy chance.
From silly hats to the dancing chore,
This space hums with love evermore.

Voices soften, then burst into glee,
Sharing our dreams like kites in a tree.
A jump, a laugh, a tickle, a shout,
In this delightful chaos, there's no doubt.

Balancing legs on the coffee table,
Mimicking stars, our hearts' own fable.
A serene moment wrapped in the fun,
Together we spark, like moon and sun.

Moments Wrapped in Warmth

Cozy blankets wrap us like a hug,
With sips of cocoa that make us tug.
Giggling fits over cheesy jokes,
As we share stories of silly blokes.

The clock ticks slow with laughter's grace,
Every chuckle fills this happy space.
From hidden snacks to secret winks,
In this warmth, our bond distinctly links.

A pop quiz on who remembers when,
Turns quite wild with exaggerated men.
Our living room bursts with playful light,
Where every shadow sparkles just right.

As the day fades, silliness remains,
Wrapped in love like soft, flowing chains.
With every squish and joyful shout,
These moments are what love's about.

Starlight Through the Windows

Underneath the blanket, a pile of snacks,
We plot our escape from the fridge's attacks.
With laughter and crumbs scattered everywhere,
We dance in the glow of the evening air.

There's chaos in cushions, a fort built anew,
My dog thinks it's chaos, we call it a zoo.
A flick of the remote, the show starts to play,
As we giggle and snack, the night slips away.

Whispers of secrets, beneath night's calm dome,
Pretending we're ninjas, while hiding from gnome.
The clock ticks in jests, time's not on our side,
But joy's in the moment, let's take it for a ride.

Each starlit giggle is stitched in the night,
As we share goofy tales, everything feels right.
Together we shine, like stars from above,
In the warmth of our haven, we'll always find love.

Silhouettes of Togetherness

The shadows shift lightly upon the old wall.
Silly poses we strike—oh, we're having a ball!
With popcorn explosions, kernels fly high,
As laughter erupts like the moon in the sky.

We start a fierce debate on who took the last slice,
Accusations of theft—not once, but thrice!
With pillows as shields, we giggle and yell,
In the battlefield of cushions, all's ringing a bell.

The world outside fades, as we bicker and tease,
Turning battles to banter, you're beguiled with ease.
As silhouettes dance like they're lost in a trance,
We fit into moments that perfectly chance.

With nighttime adventures, our laughter's the sound,
Crafting memories, both silly and profound.
In every jest shared, our hearts intertwine,
In shadows, we gather—oh, love is divine!

Cracks in the Fabric

Oh look at that squeaky, worn-out old chair,
It squeals when I sit, like it's caught in despair.
But there's comfort in quirks, every wrinkle a tale,
We laugh at its noises, like ships in a gale.

Cushions like pillows fluff up for a fight,
When I reach for the snacks, my dog thinks it's night.
An epic quest, dodging paws left and right,
In this treasure hunt, there's no need for fright.

With walls watching over, they join in the cheer,
As secrets spill forth, no judgment 'round here.
An art piece of laughter, we paint with the mess,
Finding joy in the cracks, who needs to impress?

From giggles to sighs, every moment is gold,
In this tapestry woven with stories retold.
We'll dance with our shadows, in fabric so worn,
It's here in our haven, a love reborn.

Heartfelt Stillness

In the calm of the night, a stillness so sweet,
We share goofy dreams, both sad and complete.
With a blanket cocoon and thoughts flying high,
We rewrite the stars with each heartfelt sigh.

The clock ticks away, but we don't seem to care,
As we mess up the stories, and giggle with flair.
Each murmur a secret, like whispers through air,
In this funny enclave, there's always a dare.

Sipping cocoa mixed with a sprinkle of fun,
Bringing light to our hearts, like the rise of the sun.
Mismatched jammies provide the perfect style,
As we dance in our dreams, mile after mile.

With warmth wrapped around us, the world fades away,
We're masterful artisans, in our joyous play.
As stillness surrounds, here's where laughter ignites,
In the depths of our love, the heart truly lights.

The Heart's Canvas

On the wall, a painting hung,
A cat in a hat, oh how it sung!
We laugh at the colors that clash and blend,
In this cozy haven, all troubles mend.

Socks on the floor, a rainbow parade,
Each step we take, a new charade.
With twirling chairs and dancing books,
We write our tales in playful looks.

In this space where laughter dwells,
Echoes of jokes and silly yells.
Where tea spills like stories unplanned,
And every moment feels just grand.

With laughter stains on the cushions tight,
We muse in giggles deep into night.
Each memory painted, a splash of cheer,
A masterpiece crafted, year after year.

Embracing Whimsy

Cushions piled high like a mountain range,
Every thrown pillow feels quite strange.
We giggle and tumble as the dog joins in,
A circus of chaos where fun can begin.

Sipping cocoa with marshmallows afloat,
While a cat named Whiskers commandeers the boat.
Two forks for one cake, we wouldn't dare share,
A sweet little standoff, a sugary affair.

Knotted blankets form our cozy nest,
We build silly forts, it's simply the best.
A wild dance party breaks out at noon,
With music from somewhere, maybe a cartoon.

A sprinkle of charm and a dash of glee,
Our antics weave tales as wild as the sea.
In this quirky corner, realities bend,
Where the silly and fun will never end.

Imprints on the Floor

Footprints of joy leave marks on the mat,
Confetti from parties and crumbs from the cat.
The laughter echoes from shoe to shoe,
In this floor show of memories, old and new.

Sprinklers of spritz, on a Wednesday night,
Dancing with popcorn, our spirits take flight.
The coffee spills in patterns absurd,
We embrace the chaos, without saying a word.

A game of charades on a rainy day,
Where costumes appear in the silliest way.
With socks on our hands and hats on our toes,
Each act builds a history nobody knows.

So let's stomp our feet as we make our own song,
In the midst of the mess, where we all get along.
With secret imprints telling tales of delight,
We gather our joy every morning and night.

The Charm of Us

Together we fumble, together we giggle,
A dance with the broom leaves us feeling a wiggle.
With snacks hidden deep in the couch's fold,
Each treasure discovered is precious and bold.

We try to build castles, they fall with a thud,
But our laughter is gold, like sweet peanut butter.
With games of old age, we act like we're young,
Our hearts full of mischief and songs yet unsung.

The coffee pot whistles a tune just for us,
Creating a symphony, a delicious fuss.
We toast with our mugs, clinking joyfully bright,
In this place of our making, everything feels right.

With every collected and warm-hearted glance,
This curious space leads us all to a dance.
The charm that we share, an unspoken vow,
Is captured in moments, here and right now.

Memories on the Wall

Photos of laughter hang with pride,
From goofy poses, a love we can't hide.
Every snapshot, a treasured delight,
Reminders of joy, morning to night.

Socks mismatched, a cheerful sight,
A cat in a box, what a funny plight!
With every tumble and each silly dance,
We bask in the warmth of a lively romance.

Echoes of laughter bounce off the floor,
Tales of mishaps, who could ask for more?
The couch is a stage for witty retorts,
Where banter flows freely, a game of sports.

In this gallery, our quirks take flight,
Creating a canvas of pure delight.
We wait for new moments, more tales to unfold,
In this hallowed space where we're brave and bold.

Harmonies of a Shared Space

In our cozy nook, tunes are composed,
From voices that crack, and laughter exposed.
The fridge hums along, a chorus divine,
While pets join the song in perfect align.

Hiccups and howls, no rhythm in sight,
Yet each note rings out, it feels just right.
The kettle's a drummer, the chairs sway to beat,
A symphony crafted from every heartbeat.

Pillow fights break out, a spontaneous jam,
As we twist and we twirl, oh who gives a damn?
In this vibrant space where quirks intertwine,
We dance to the music, your heart next to mine.

As our lives intertwine, we strum with glee,
Each note a reminder of what's yet to be.
With the love we share, all harmonies blend,
A whimsical orchestration, no need to pretend.

Radiance of Togetherness

In the glow of evening, we gather round,
Bathed in a light that's warm and profound.
The snacks are aplenty, the laughter flows free,
As we playfully bicker, who's winning? Not me!

The cat finds a perch on the snack table high,
As we dodge little paws, with a frustrated sigh.
But this kind of chaos, oh what sheer delight,
Our clumsy misfortune makes every night bright.

The TV reveals our favorite show,
With rolling eyes and popcorn in tow.
We cheer at the plot twists, then groan at the style,
United in madness, we've made it our file.

Amidst all the banter, the giggles and grins,
The light that we share is where the fun begins.
With hearts full of radiance, our spirits ignite,
In this cherished cocoon, everything feels right.

Threads of Affection

In our haven of quirks, love's threads intertwine,
Stitching together those moments divine.
With mismatched cushions and laughter that grows,
We craft our own fabric from joys and from woes.

Each blanket a story, each throw a delight,
We cuddle and tease as we cuddle so tight.
The pet sneaks a snack while we're deep in our game,
His fur coat a reminder, we're all quite the same.

Silly inside jokes, oh how they do fly,
With puns and wisecracks as we make our way by.
The world feels so cozy, so utterly bright,
As we wrap ourselves in this love-laced sight.

Through the threads of our laughter, we weave a fine tale,

Where smiles are the fabric and love never fails.
Not just a shared space, but a tapestry spun,
In this vibrant realm, we laugh, we have fun.

The Quilt of Shared Memories

Each patch a joke, a giggle, a cheer,
A tangle of threads that holds us near.
The colors are bright, like our laughter shared,
In this cozy space, we are always paired.

Dad's snoring bass, Mom's high-pitched glee,
A symphony of chaos, as fine as can be.
We blanket ourselves in stories and dreams,
With every stitch, the quilt softly beams.

Grandma's slipped in a wink and a grin,
We gather 'round here, let the fun begin!
Unraveling tales, with a sprinkle of jest,
In this patchwork of love, we're truly blessed.

So let's curl up tight, with popcorn in hand,
To lean on each other—this is our land.
In laughter's embrace, we'll dance through the night,
This quilt of our lives, a warm, joyful sight.

Aroma of Home-cooked Love

In the kitchen, chaos, the smells swirl and dance,
Spaghetti flops, but we all take a chance.
Garlic erupts like a small rocket's flight,
Each meal is a gamble, who'll win the fight?

Mom's secret sauce? It's really just luck,
A sprinkle of cinnamon, a dash or a cluck.
Cooking together, a recipe's bliss,
But mostly it's laughter that's served with a kiss.

Dad's culinary skills are a rumor, I think,
Last night's endeavor was far from pink!
But when we sit down, it flavors the soul,
Love baked in each dish, that's our ultimate goal.

So raise up a glass to the feast that we've made,
In this aromatic chaos, our fears start to fade.
Together we munch, and together we giggle,
In the kitchen of memories, we happily wiggle.

Cushioned Conversations

On this well-loved couch, we tumble and tease,
Where raucous debates flow like a cool breeze.
Pillows are thrown, and laughter can soar,
When a jest turns to chaos, we can't help but roar.

Each cushion a throne, our kingdom of glee,
In our bouncy realm, where we all can agree.
Trading silly stories of heart and of head,
From awkward school dances to dreams in their bed.

Sofa wars happen, who gets the best seat?
With giggles and screams, we reclaim our defeat.
A fort made of laughter, a blanket to wrap,
In this silly space, there's no need to nap.

So here's to our chatter, a sweet, tangled mess,
With whispers and giggles, we banish all stress.
In our cushioned domain, let the good times unfurl,
This laughter-filled haven is our bright, happy world.

Finding Peace in the Present

In the heart of chaos, we find our own calm,
With tickles and hugs, oh what a charm!
Messy hair days become treasured delight,
In the moment we're bound, everything feels right.

Sipping on tea, keeping tabs on the guess,
Is it sugar and cream, or just a bit less?
Nostalgia tickles, like a feather's soft touch,
In stillness we gather, we adore it so much.

Let's pause for a while, let the laughter roll in,
With the warmth of our stories, we let the day spin.
The clock's just a joker playing tricks on our sips,
Time laughs as we linger, savoring these trips.

So here in this moment, let's cherish the fun,
With friends and with family, the laughter's not done.
Finding peace in the giggle, love wrapped all around,
In this patchwork of fun, our joy is profound.

Growth Under the Hearth

In corners where dust bunnies roam,
Laughter sprouts like plants in a dome.
Socks go missing, duties forgot,
Here's where we dream, oh what a lot!

Crumbs beneath the ever-worn chair,
Secret exchanges float on the air.
We giggle and snack, it's a grand buffet,
In our messy abode, we love every day!

Old board games hiding, gathering dust,
With dice in hand, oh, who can we trust?
Silly bets traded with colorful flair,
Moments so goofy, life's real debonair!

Under this roof, we bloom and play,
In a tapestry woven of magical sway.
Laughter's the fertilizer, smiles our sun,
Where shadows of troubles simply run.

Frames of Forever

Snapshots of laughter, faces aglow,
In frames stacked high, like life's little show.
Goofy poses, and hats askew,
Each picture's a memory, cherished and true.

Captured in time, our quirkiest bit,
Grandfather's dance, oh, we all admit!
Necklaces of pasta, and cupcakes with flair,
Gold dusts of chaos, we just don't care!

Here in this gallery, time twists and bends,
From kitten-faced joys to playful amends
Every photo, a chapter, our story unfolds,
In vibrant silliness, our love never grows old!

With each click, another jest we weave,
In frames of laughter, we dare to believe.
Moments so funny, they dance all around,
In this gallery of love, happiness found!

The Rhythm of Together

Bouncing to music, we shimmied and shook,
Each silly step, like a well-loved book.
We twist and we twirl, in our little space,
Finding the beat in a wobbly race!

The couch is a stage, with pillows as props,
We hop on the sofa, a symphony of flops.
Rhythmic giggles bounce off the walls,
As we let our hearts dance, whoever recalls!

With socks for our shoes, we stomp and we slide,
Floating on laughter, companions collide.
Each clap and a cheer, ignites such delight,
In this joyous chaos, we dance through the night!

Together, we spin in a whirl of our own,
A melody sweet, in this silly bone zone.
With every laugh, the world fades away,
It's the rhythm of spirit that makes our hearts sway!

Love Letters and Souvenirs

In crumpled notes, our wishes reside,
Hidden in cushions, like secrets, they hide.
Caught in the projects, great schemes we make,
With stickers and crayons, oh what a cake!

Souvenirs collected, like quirky old hats,
Each telling a story, of capers and spats.
From mismatched mugs to spoons of great cheer,
Every item a tale, laughter draws near!

A postcard from Vegas, a weird souvenir,
Reminds us of mischief, and endless good cheer.
From travels in dreams, we bring back the fun,
In love's little trinkets, adventures begun!

Beneath a night sky where wishes run wild,
Who needs perfection when love is the child?
With laughter as ink, and joy as the thread,
In these letters and tokens, our hearts are well fed!

Swaying in Sync

Two chairs dance, both quite a sight,
With popcorn tossed, oh what a night!
The dog joins in, a furry delight,
As we all laugh, hearts feeling light.

A game of cards, we play with flair,
Cheating a bit? Well, who'd declare?
The raccoon mask that I wear,
Brings giggles echoing, filling the air.

With cushions piled in a crazy mess,
Who knew such chaos could bring such zest?
As pillows fly, we feel so blessed,
In our private circus, we jest and jest.

Then the lights dim, our laughter's tune,
Watching cartoons under the moon.
With every chuckle, we're over the moon,
In our cozy haven, we find our swoon.

Dialogues of the Heart

A whispered word, a playful tease,
You steal a fry, but I just freeze.
With munching sounds, our hearts appease,
In every chuckle, love's magic flees.

"Your hair looks like a bird's nest!" I shout,
You throw a pillow all about.
But in this chaos, without a doubt,
These silly moments, they're what life's about.

A dance-off starts with lopsided moves,
Feet all tripping, the laughter grooves.
With silly hats, our spirit improves,
Together in rhythm, our joy concludes.

Through playful banter, our bond we weave,
In every jest, we choose to believe.
With giggly whispers, we never grieve,
In dialogues sweet, we shall achieve.

Pillows of Peace

A fortress built of cushions tall,
Each pillow stuffed, we have a ball.
Inside this hideout, we'll never fall,
Our laughter resonates, echoing call.

With mismatched socks, we sit and grin,
The cat's our referee, wanting to win.
As we throw snacks, let the games begin,
In this cozy space, fun's always in.

A knock-knock joke, a pun so bad,
You roll your eyes, but still, you're glad.
In our little nest, we forget the sad,
With each silly moment, we feel so rad.

As night descends, we hold our breath,
In soft blanket forts, we conquer death.
With whispered dreams, our hearts bequeath,
In pillowed embrace, we find our heft.

Resplendence of Us

In our small realm, where giggles reign,
You spill your drink—oh, such disdain!
But laughter rises, eclipsing the pain,
   In every blunder, love will sustain.

A movie night becomes a brawl,
With popcorn flyin', it's the best of all.
Your dramatic gasp, your wild thrall,
Make every scene a hilarious call.

With dance moves that could start a trend,
We twirl and spin—but never bend.
This joyous chaos, it feels like a blend,
Of warmth and laughter that will not end.

At day's retreat, we toss and play,
Creating memories in our own way.
As night envelopes, we softly sway,
In resplendent moments, love's here to stay.

www.ingramcontent.com/pod-product-compliance
Lightning Source LLC
Chambersburg PA
CBHW060140230426
43661CB00003B/499

Original title:
A Hat for Every Story

Copyright © 2025 Creative Arts Management OÜ
All rights reserved.

Author: Nora Sinclair
ISBN HARDBACK: 978-1-80586-123-2
ISBN PAPERBACK: 978-1-80586-595-7

Portraits Under a Brim

A fedora perched with flair,
Sparks giggles in the air.
Top hats wobbling, oh so grand,
Each a tale, a life unplanned.

Bowler hats with secret charms,
Whispering of dubious farms.
Funky caps with colors bright,
Dance around, a sheer delight.

Sun hats sharing precious news,
While silly wigs get all the views.
Every brim holds laughter tight,
In the sun or moon's soft light.

The Vault of Velvet Visors

In the vault where visions sleep,
Velvet caps with secrets keep.
A pirate's hat with golden flair,
Promised riches, made to share.

Sombreros in a playful row,
Winking tales of long ago.
A baseball cap with pizza scent,
Reminds us where the time was spent.

Cowboy hats with playful spins,
Chasing dust and all our sins.
Each a treasure, bold and bold,
Drawing stories, young and old.

Memories in Millinery

A floppy hat from sunny days,
Hides the laughter, soft sun rays.
In a beanie, warmth takes hold,
A thousand giggles yet untold.

A beret with a sassy flair,
Hides the thoughts that dance in air.
Each a snippet of delight,
Worn in fragments, day or night.

A cap adorned with silly pins,
Whispers tales of silly sins.
In every fold, a story's spun,
With giggles, each day is won.

Adventures Under a Wide Brim

Under   brim, adventures roam,
A hat that calls, feels like home.
An explorer's cap with maps in folds,
Stories of treasure and fortunes bold.

Sun hats guiding through the sun,
Finding laughter, endless fun.
Shady shades with crafty seams,
Capture all our wildest dreams.

A fisherman's cap with tales to spin,
Of giant catches, where to begin?
Each wide brim a stage to play,
Making memories every day.

Threads of Identity

On my head, a crown of cheese,
Made from crackers, if you please!
With every snack, I feel so grand,
A cheesy prince, rule my snack land.

A beanie topped with googly eyes,
It wobbles with my every sigh.
It sees the world, it gives a wink,
Together, we both boldly think.

The Stories We Wear

A wizard's hat made of a mop,
It makes my inner magic hop.
I cast my spells with broomstick grace,
Home-cooked magic, what a taste!

A sombrero for the sun's bright glare,
Decorated with a rubber bear.
Together we dance under sun's rays,
Mixing laughs in silly ways.

Tales Topped with Flourish

A top hat holds my dreams so wide,
Does it have rabbits? Ignore my pride!
I pull out snacks, my hungry friends,
Where more will this hat's journey end?

A baseball cap with jokes galore,
Each joke hits like a playful score.
With laughter's help, we hit the field,
The humor's punch, our wins revealed.

Whims and Whirls of Headgear

I wear a beret made of whipped cream,
Fashion's sweet, it feels like a dream.
With every scoop, a giggle spills,
A dessert hat, it surely thrills!

An astronaut helmet, cardboard chic,
Launch me to space, gravity weak.
Stars are jokes that twinkle bright,
In this universe, joy takes flight.

Lids of Legacy

A giant sombrero, bold and bright,
Hides a taco party, what a sight!
An astronaut's cap, so puffy and round,
Launches jokes that are lost and found.

A wizard's hat with a pointy peak,
Holds spells for laughs, but it may squeak!
An antique bowler, classy and neat,
Turns a catwalk into a street.

A baseball cap brings sunny play,
While quirky styles invite ballet.
Each lid a clue to stories untold,
Where laughter blooms, brave and bold.

Narrative Nooks

In a cozy nook, a beanie waits,
For tales of mischief and dinner plates.
A fedora whispers of secrets past,
As all the giggles and stories amassed.

Beneath a sunhat, adventures grow,
With lemonade dreams and a bug-eyed show.
A chef's hat puffs with culinary jokes,
While aprons add spice to the mix of folks.

So grab your lid, let joy ignite,
In every nook, laughter takes flight.
From casual chats to wild capers,
Each hat crafts stories of starry drapers.

The Canopy of Characters

In a tree of hats, a jester swings,
Wearing colors bright, he freely sings.
A crown atop a quirky clown,
Sprinkles smiles all over town.

An explorer's cap carries tales of old,
Of dragons slain and treasure bold.
While a hardhat hums of construction cheer,
Building laughter year after year.

An elf hat twirls with magical flair,
Spreading giggles everywhere!
Beneath this canopy, stories unite,
Each character's quirk brings pure delight.

Hats, Histories, and Hues

A top hat tricks with a magic flair,
Pulling out rabbits from thin air!
A sun hat giggles in summer's breeze,
Sharing secrets with the buzzing bees.

An aviator cap boasts of the sky,
Where dreams take flight, oh my, oh my!
While a sailor's hat spins yarns of the sea,
With nautical dreams for you and me.

Each color tells a tale anew,
From rosy cheeks to skies so blue.
With every hat, a dance begins,
In hats we trust, where joy never thins.

Charmed by the Chapeau

In a shop where the oddities dwell,
A cap with a tale, oh, can you tell?
It danced on the shelf, cheerful and spry,
A wink from its button, a glimmering eye.

A beanie that whispers sweet secrets of pie,
A top hat that giggles and dares you to fly.
With each quirky piece, the laughter will swell,
For every fine chapeau has a story to sell.

The Legacy Hosted by Headgear

There once was a helmet with stories galore,
Of knights and of dragons, and battles of yore.
It squeaked every time someone wore it with pride,
And echoed the tales of adventures worldwide.

A beret adorned with graffiti and flair,
Told tales of a painter who once rocked the scuare.
Each stitch and each thread held a giggle and grin,
A legacy worn on the head and the chin.

Secrets Beneath the Brim

A wide-brimmed hat with a penchant for schemes,
Hid secrets of magicians, and wild, daring dreams.
It swirled up some laughter, a trick or a ruse,
With a flick of its fabric, it started to cruise.

Beneath the bold fringe of a straw sunlit hat,
A sarcastic voice crooned, 'Ain't this just the cat?'
With each twirl and flip, mystery spun tight,
Unraveling tales by the dim candlelight.

Whimsical Weavings

A knitted cap with an odd little curl,
Spun stories of friendship in a topsy-turvy whirl.
It cheered at the antics of jesters so spry,
And snickered with glee as the pigeons did fly.

In patches and colors, there lay a sweet dream,
Of joyous parades and an ice cream-themed scheme.
Each tale stitched in laughter, a yarn full of cheer,
For every fine weaver knows joy brings us near.

The Silhouette of Storytelling

In a room full of tales, where laughter rolls,
The chef wears a toque, while the jester sprawls.
A pirate twirls a bandana with flair,
While the frog in a top hat croaks dreams in the air.

With every twist and turn, the plot gets wild,
A cowboy's at the bar, tipsy and styled.
The detective's in shadows, a tweed cap so neat,
While the cat in the bowler scampers on feet.

A witch in her bonnet stirs bubbles and brew,
While the fairy in feathers giggles her cue.
Each silhouette dancing, a comical sight,
In the theater of life, where tales take flight.

So gather your stories, both silly and bright,
For every character's laugh adds joy to the night.
With hats of all shapes, from silly to grand,
In the silhouette of stories, together we stand.

Veils of Mystique

In a carnival booth, the mystic's unveiled,
A magician appears with a grin that's scaled.
A lady in lace, her hat tilted high,
Whispers secrets to the zany butterfly.

The clown with a bowler, so round and so red,
Juggles umbrellas right over your head.
The gypsy in feathers reads fortune with flair,
While a walrus in goggles rolls by with a stare.

Disguises and laughter, they dance in the night,
With veils woven softly, a whimsical sight.
Everyone's hiding behind something fun,
As tales start to mingle, the night's just begun.

So peek through the veils, embrace the delight,
Where every strange hat shines vivid and bright.
With laughter as currency, we trade and we blend,
In this carnival of stories, where fun never ends.

A Symphony of Silhouettes

Under the moon, a parade takes its stage,
Each figure adorned in a whimsical page.
The conductor, a penguin with feathers so grand,
Leads a band of characters, hats held in hand.

A scarecrow with a sombrero hops to the beat,
While the snail in a top hat moves in slow heat.
The mermaid in sequins splashes with cheer,
As the shadows of laughter swoop down from the sphere.

The notes blend and sway as the stories unfold,
In a symphony stitched from the shy and the bold.
Each silhouette twirls, a dance full of glee,
In this quirky ensemble, we all can be free.

So tap to the rhythm of the hats being worn,
In the symphony of tales, laughter is born.
Join in the frolic, let go of regret,
In this joyous parade, there's no need to fret.

The Quest for the Perfect Lid

In search of a lid for each fable untold,
A wizard in beanies, oh, so bold.
An elf with a visor dreams big as the moon,
While a dragon in slippers starts humming a tune.

With bountiful boxes of fedoras galore,
A clown tries a beret, then tumbles to floor.
A pirate in pigtails yells, 'Where's me crown?'
In the quest for the lid, they tumble around.

The gnome with a helmet is planning to race,
While a ghost in a bonnet carves out his space.
Each headpiece a story, a giggle, a cheer,
On this quest for a lid, the fun is so near.

So grab at the options, don't wear just one,
In the tale of the hat, we bask in the fun.
For every new story, a new hat to fit,
In our quest for perfection, we say, 'Never quit!'

Lids that Whisper Legends

In the cupboard, a fedora waits,
Holding secrets of long-lost fates.
With every tilt, it spins a yarn,
Of daring deeds and fields of corn.

A beanie dreams of snowy nights,
Where snowmen dance and snowball fights.
With a pom-pom bright atop its dome,
It tells of frolics far from home.

A top hat waits with elegance,
Whispering of a magician's chance.
With a flourish, it pulls out a rabbit,
And a dancing duck that loves to habit.

So many lids with stories to share,
Each one a character, bold and rare.
With chuckles and gasps, they capture us,
In a world of whimsy, oh so wondrous.

The Cloak of Curiosities

A cloak woven with threads of giggles,
Where oddities bounce and wiggle.
Each pocket filled with odd delights,
From rubber chickens to birthday lights.

A cape that flutters with a flair,
Telling tales of the cats that dare.
To sneak and prance through the midnight air,
With ribbons of mischief trailing where.

A shawl adorned with quirky charms,
Whispers of frogs and magical farms.
With a twist and a twirl, oh what a sight,
As the stories unfold in the glow of night.

Wrap it snug and let it speak,
Of whimsical wonders, oh so unique.
In this cloak of quirks, we all align,
As laughter bubbles and stars align.

Adornments of the Mind

A bowler hat with a crooked grin,
Hiding dreams where the joy begins.
It hops right off and starts to prance,
Inviting all for a silly dance.

A sunhat filled with the brightest rays,
Sends forth laughter in all its ways.
It shields from clouds that want to frown,
And encourages smiles all around.

A crown of daisies, cheeky and bold,
With tales of fairies and treasures untold.
It's a tiara for the jesters' parade,
Celebrating quirks, unafraid.

Adorn yourself and join the play,
In this realm where laughter stays.
With headgear that dances, spins and jives,
Stories thrive where the funny thrives.

Curved Crowns and Timeless Tales

A pirate's hat with a feather plume,
Holds treasures hidden in every room.
It shouts of ships and waves that crash,
Of buried gold and a daring dash.

A jester's cap with bells aglow,
Tells the tales of a fizzy show.
With every jingle, it spins a line,
Of silly antics and punchlines divine.

A wizard's hat, pointy and grand,
Conducts a symphony of laugh and band.
It conjures giggles from far and wide,
With every spell, there's no need to hide.

So come and wear these quirky crowns,
And summon laughter in leaps and bounds.
In every twist and every tale,
You'll find the joy that never fails.

Epics in Every Stitch

In a world where fabric dreams,
A knight's cap giggles and gleams.
With every stitch, a story winks,
Of dragon tea and pirate drinks.

There's a hat that dances with glee,
A floppy thing named Mystery.
It twists and twirls on heads awry,
While making cat jokes passing by.

A ruler's crown that doubles as cat,
Worn by kings who love to chat.
Each gem is a pun in disguise,
Those royal snickers are no surprise.

Behold the jester's floppy crown,
With bells that jingle upside-down.
He tells of queens who bake with glee,
And jesters who plot their grand spree.

Imaginary Fables of Fabric

A sun hat boasts of golden rays,
With tales of long-forgotten days.
It whispers secrets of the breeze,
And laughs at clowns who trip on leaves.

A beanie dreams of snowy nights,
Where snowmen wear their juggling tights.
Each purl and stitch, a giggle grows,
As frostbit fingers toe the nose.

A top hat filled with rabbits' quips,
Unravels tales of magic trips.
With every leap, a laugh resounds,
As vaudeville antics spin in bounds.

The bucket hat holds water's tales,
Of fishing lines and sailor's gales.
With each splash, the fish do grin,
While tales of tides and waves begin.

The Tapestry of Tales

In a room where all hats collide,
A wild adventure now must ride.
Each fabric tells a joke or jest,
From floppy ears, to feathered crest.

The sombrero spins wild fables,
Of fiesta times and dancing tables.
With every twirl, a taco flies,
As laughter echoes through the skies.

A beret sighs with perfume grace,
Of artists lost in time and space.
Each stroke of color, bright and bold,
Brings giggles wrapped in stories old.

A hard hat speaks of silly falls,
Of construction sites and leaky walls.
With every clasp and twist of fate,
It laughs at all who hesitate.

Hats That Recite Poetry

A fedora hums a rhythmic tune,
Of midnight walks beneath the moon.
With every tip, a stanza's spun,
As lively laughter's just begun.

A paper hat reads silly notes,
Of pirate vows on tiny boats.
Each crease and fold, a giggling verse,
With clues to treasure, or maybe worse.

The newsboy cap, with tales to tell,
Recites the daily, odd, and swell.
With every snap, it flings a rhyme,
Of headlines warped in playful time.

An astronaut's helmet dreams in flight,
Of comets who dance in the night.
It spins around with cosmic glee,
As space adventures flow carefree.

The Charmed Headspace

In a quirky shop where hats abound,
A wizard's cap spun round and round.
A jester's cap with bells that cling,
Makes everyone dance, it's a silly thing.

An astronaut's helmet, snug and tight,
Makes you feel like taking flight.
A chef's toque high on a head,
Turns each meal into a tale, well-spread.

A pirate's tri-corner makes you shout,
'Yo ho, matey!' as you prance about.
Each hat holds laughter, don't you see?
In this wild place, we're all set free.

Caps of Colorful Chronicles

A beanie of blue for the cool, cool days,
Hold tight to dreams in a whimsical maze.
A baseball cap with a goofy grin,
Adds a little fun to the league of kin.

A top hat towering, with style galore,
Winks to the world, 'There's always more '
The sun hat whispers, 'Let's lounge and read',
In this garden of colors, we plant a seed.

The cowboy hat tips, with a twirl and spin,
Every cowboy's tale starts with a grin.
Caps of all hues, each with a lore,
Join us in laughter, there's always more!

Layers of Narrative

Under every layer, a story hides,
A fedora that swings, as adventure rides.
A sun helmet giggles at the sweltering heat,
While snowcaps tease with a frosty beat.

A beret perched with an artist's flair,
Whispers of colors that dance in the air.
A crown of paper, we're kings for a day,
In this layer of fun, we laugh and play.

Each style, each tale, a treasure to wear,
Fashion's a riddle, but Who really cares?
For underneath it all, we're young at heart,
In this layer of laughter, we make our art.

The Many Faces of Headwear

A cap with a visor, tilted just right,
Turns a mundane trip into a flight.
A sombrero that dreams of far-off lands,
Makes every salsa feel like soft sands.

A baker's hat, fluffy and sweet,
Makes every kitchen turn up the heat.
A traffic cone, silly on your head,
Directs the fun where it needs to spread.

Every face brightens with a new design,
From floppy hats to top hats, in the sunshine.
In this fashion of giggles, silly and bold,
With the many faces, a tale unfolds.

The Essence in Every Crown

In the cupboard, a crown unworn,
With feathers and sparkles, it's quite the thorn.
A prince once wore it, claimed he was grand,
But tripped on a shoe, fell flat on the sand.

A wizard's old hat, with a magical twist,
Made him look fancy, impossible to resist.
But every time he'd cast, oh what a blunder,
His socks vanished first, amidst all the thunder.

The cap of a jester, so bright and quirky,
Made children laugh, though his jokes were murky.
With bells that jingled, he'd prance around,
Yet slipped on a peel, tumbled to the ground.

So many hats, such curious tales,
Each with a moment where humor prevails.
From crowns to caps, all forms of glee,
In life's silly play, there's a hat for thee.

Legends Under Layered Cloth

The wrestler's hat, a championship feat,
Claimed victory, but slipped on his feet.
Dressed for the brawl, he yelled with pride.
Then fell for a duck, his honor denied.

A cook's puffy cap, so lofty and tall,
He sprinkled the spice, felt ten feet tall.
But when he flipped pancakes, a tiny misfire,
Dripped syrup on guests, they laughed at his flyer.

The pirate's old tricorn, with tales of the sea,
Swore up and down he was fierce and free.
Yet when faced with a parrot, squawking and bold,
He squealed like a girl, fell back on the cold.

Through every adventure, from dastardly duds,
Legends arise in laughter and floods.
Each hat holds a tale, a giggle or cheer,
Beneath layered cloth, mischief is near.

The Bundled Stories of Hats

A detective's fedora, so sharp and slick,
Off to solve riddles, he felt quite the trick.
But peering too close at a cupcake's design,
His hat dipped in frosting, oh how it did shine!

The gardener's sun hat, with flowers galore,
Promised to bloom, but then came a bore.
As bugs found a home, living under the brims,
He sneezed with delight, oh, how the light dims!

A helmet of knight, so shiny and bright,
Claimed to protect in the fiercest of fights.
Yet while jousting whales, he slipped on a shell,
He laughed so hard, he forgot he could fell.

Every hat tells a story, with humor concealed,
From wild, frolicking tales, each fate is revealed.
So gather your hats, and let's share a laugh,
In the bundles of stories, we'll dance on this path.

Weaving Whimsy

In a town where hats run free,
Silly shapes climb every tree.
Jesters jump with floppy ears,
While wizards wear their puffed-up spheres.

A rabbit dons a top hat tall,
While penguins strut in beak-like sprawl.
Each headpiece tells a tale so bright,
Of fables woven in pure delight.

Grasshoppers hop in bowlers neat,
While clowns parade with dancing feet.
Frogs in fedoras croak with glee,
Each stitch a laugh, a jubilee.

So grab a cap or snatch a crown,
Join the fun in this wild town.
For every hat has character,
Each quirky tale a new narrator!

Of Brims and Beliefs

In a world of caps and whimsical dreams,
Where even the lampposts sport funny seams.
A sombrero spins on a snail's soft shell,
Telling stories that only it can tell.

A beanie whispers secrets of cold,
While a sunhat gleams, oh so bold.
Each rim and angle might cause a laugh,
As hats trot around like they're on a path.

Pirates wear tricorns made of cheese,
While hippos sport hats that sway in the breeze.
Every headpiece sets the stage,
For zany tales that engage.

So plop on a hat and spin your yarn,
For who knows what stories may be born?
In this merry land of whimsy and mirth,
Each hat is a treasure, a joyous rebirth!

The Headwear Harmony

Fashion a bonanza, a whimsical sight,
Where hats play the music, day and night.
A top hat twirls with a tap-dancing shoe,
While a beret sings of Paris in blue.

Bowties and bonnets join in the groove,
Each piece of headwear has got the move.
Scarves join the band, swaying with flair,
Creating a ruckus, oh what a pair!

Sun hats flap with a jazzy beat,
As goofballs bust out in silly repeat.
Fedora flicks the baton with grace,
Each note a giggle in this hat-wearing race.

So let's all join in this dapper affair,
Pick any ensemble, we truly don't care.
For in this harmony of quirky delight,
Every hat spins a tale, oh so light!

Kaleidoscope of Caps

In a shop filled with colors, bright as can be,
Hats waltz around, so carefree.
A rainbow cap laughs at its friend,
A bearded bonnet with tales to send.

Unicorn horns twirl with zest,
While arriving in goggles, a chicken's dressed!
Every brim bobs in a quirky parade,
Providing the joy that'll never fade.

Each piece tells stories of lands far away,
Of pirates, of knights, in a fanciful play.
A cap of pancakes makes everyone cheer,
As syrupy laughter fills the air near.

So put on a crown or clamber with flair,
In this whimsical world, hats are everywhere!
For each headpiece a journey, a patchwork of fun,
In this lively display, the laughter's just begun!

The Brim of Imagination

Upon my head, a giant cheese,
It wobbles when I bend my knees.
With crackers stacked in perfect rows,
I dream of feasts, where laughter flows.

A crown of feathers, bright and bold,
Makes every tale amusingly told.
I strut around like feathered queen,
Imagination reigns, so keen.

With a top hat filled with dancing mice,
I tell my friends, 'They fix my spice!'
Each whimsy atop my head so grand,
Is ready for a funny band.

So gather 'round for stories bright,
Each headpiece brings such pure delight.
In every cap, a giggle hides,
Join in the fun, let joy abide.

Tipped Toward Adventure

A helmet made of jellybeans,
I ride a bike through candy scenes.
Each pedal makes a sour sound,
As flavors burst and spin around.

An astronaut's cap, so high and wide,
Takes me to space on a chocolate slide.
Floating past stars of whipped cream fluff,
I bounce through cosmos, laughing tough.

A pirate's patch, all worn and frayed,
Yarrr! With treasure maps displayed.
I sail my ship on cola seas,
With gummy bears and licorice trees.

So tip your hat to fanciful fun,
Adventure awaits for everyone.
In whimsical hats, we few unite,
With laughter and tales that feel just right.

Headpieces of Change

A fedora spun from pasta twirls,
With spaghetti strands that dance and swirls.
I twirl it like a magic wand,
And pasta spirits form a band.

A beanie with a motor's buzz,
Makes me the coolest, just because.
I zoom around on roller skates,
With laughter echoing, laughter waits.

A wizard's cap of sparkling light,
Turns every frown into delight.
With just a flick, I change my fate,
From silly to grand, oh how I rate!

In every headpiece, magic gleams,
Transforming life from cozy dreams.
So wear your crown, embrace the strange.
For life is fun with headpieces of change.

From Beanies to Berets

Sporting a beanie, snug and tight,
I roll the snowballs, gleeful sight.
With each toss, they fly so high,
Snowmen smile as I pass by.

A beret perched at a jaunty angle,
Makes me a poet with words to dangle.
I spout my verses, oh, so wise,
Yet trip on rhymes, much to my surprise.

A straw hat worn on sunny days,
Covers my thoughts in whimsical ways.
I sip my drink with extra flair,
While birds in trees join in the air.

From beanies to berets, styles collide,
Each piece of headgear, a wild ride.
So wear what brings a chuckle bright,
And savor laughter, pure delight!

The Curly Q of Curiosity

In a town where hats are quite the trend,
Curly hats twist, with no need to mend.
Each swirl and spin brings laughter near,
Curiosity grows when hats appear.

A purple hat with a floppy side,
Squeaks like a toy, what fun to ride!
The folks all gather, giggles ensue,
Curly Q caps bring joy anew.

A tall hat prances, dancing like mad,
Waving to all, it's simply a fad.
With every step, it bounces and hops,
Curly cap capers that never stop!

So twirl your hats and share a grin,
For every silly twist invites you in.
In this town, joy is here to stay,
Curly hats rule the fun parade!

Doodles in Feathered Hats

In a corner cafe, with doodles afloat,
Feathered creations spin like a boat.
A hat with a beak, laughs with delight,
It quacks and wiggles, quite the sight!

One with a rabbit, plush and round,
Hops up and down, making quite the sound.
A doodle parade, so absurdly grand,
Feathered friends join, hand in hand.

A polka dot marvel spins through the air,
Daring the others without a care.
It dances on heads, a sight to behold,
These feathered creations, stories unfold!

When laughter erupts, the doodles unite,
Creating a chaos, pure and bright.
In this quirky shop, where whimsy won't quit,
Feathered doodles always make a hit!

A Gallery of Gossamer Dreams

In a gallery lined with hats galore,
Gossamer dreams linger, wanting more.
A cap made of clouds drifts gently by,
Brightening up the dullest sky.

An artist's beret, splattered and bold,
Tells tales of colors, deep and old.
A floppy sunhat, with ribbons so bright,
Whispers secrets of a starry night.

A top hat prances, dapper and spry,
With a wink and a nod, it catches the eye.
Each fabric and feather carries a tale,
In this gallery, silliness prevails!

So step right up and try on a dream,
In gossamer hats, let laughter gleam.
These magical marvels, whimsical schemes,
Bring joy to life with their playful beams!

The Headgear Diaries

Once there was a diary, hats were the stars,
With doodles and sketches of fancy bazaars.
A sombrero with snacks, oh what a treat,
Every story bubbling, life can't be beat!

A beanie that giggles whenever it's worn,
Hilarity ensues, with every adorn.
A helmet with typing, quick as a whip,
Records the laughter, not a single blip!

In this headgear tale, oh what a mix,
With talents galore stemming from tricks.
The journal fills up, page after page,
Each hat has a voice, let loose your sage!

So embrace your headwear, let stories flow,
In the diaries of laughter, let your joy grow.
For each silly hat has a tale of its own,
Crowning the fun, wherever you roam!

The Storyteller's Shade

Under the brim, tales unfold,
Laughter and mischief, bright and bold.
A patchwork of dreams, colors collide,
With every stitch, a giggle is tied.

A cap for the jester, a crown for the queen,
Twirling scandals, all fit for the scene.
Whimsical whispers, they dance in the air,
In this shade, joy's always aware.

The Crown of Constellations

Stars on my head, what a sight to behold,
Each twinkle a story, waiting to be told.
A galaxy woven in threads of delight,
With laughter as fuel, we shine through the night.

A beanie of dreams, a turban of flair,
From sappy to silly, it's all in the air.
Each tale is a spark, each giggle a star,
In the crown of constellations, we travel afar.

Layers of Lore

Stripes and polka dots, oh what a sight,
I wear my stories, left and right.
A bucket full of giggles, a beanie of glee,
Each layer a giggle, each story a spree.

From pirates to poodles, so silly and bright,
In my jaunty old hat, I find pure delight.
With every new tale, the laughter just grows,
A fountain of fun, as everyone knows.

Brims of Beauty

Wide brims full of laughter, oh what a place,
Where jokes float around in a whimsical space.
From feathered caps to a wizard's tall hat,
Each one holds a grin, like a soft fuzzy cat.

In the snazzy parade, the stories just pop,
A flamboyant chapeau makes the humor non-stop.
With topsy-turvy tales, we all spin around,
In the brims of beauty, joy always is found.

The Pondered Peak

Atop a hill, a hat did sit,
It swayed and danced, a little bit.
A feathered friend peeked 'round the bend,
Said, "This is fun! Let's not pretend!"

With every gust, the brim would twirl,
A sight that made the whole world whirl.
They giggled loud, the duo shared,
That hat was bold, and they weren't scared!

A squirrel approached, a curious fellow,
He wore a cap of bright green mallow.
"Let's plan a party, we'll show our flair!"
And soon enough, they filled the air!

From twinkling lights to snacks galore,
Each critter came, never a bore.
A hat for laughs, a hat for cheer,
In moments bright, they held it dear.

Episodes in Embellishment

In a case of hats, a story brewed,
With polka dots and colors skewed.
A top hat twitched, a beanie grinned,
What tales would soon be pinned!

A cowboy hat, quite bold and wide,
Claimed, "I'm here for the wild ride!"
While sun hats whispered, "Stay real cool!"
The bobbled beanie was quite the fool!

"Let's swap our tales!" the fedora said,
"From lands of green to skies of red!"
With laughter echoing loud and clear,
Each hat spun yarns, we'd sit and cheer!

From wizards casting spells on nights,
To pirates planning silly fights.
Each tale was wild, each yarn was spun,
With every laugh, the hats had fun!

The Crowned Chronicles

A king's grand crown sat stacked with caps,
Each one whispered, through giggles and claps.
A jester laughed, his hat askew,
"Every crown tells tales, it's true!"

A knight in armor, looking so grand,
Bore a helmet from a far-off land.
"A battle fought for pizza's pride,
But I just found a place to hide!"

The princess beamed in her fancy hat,
"I rule the garden; come share a chat!"
With sparkling gems and bows that flowed.
She ruled with joy; her heart, it glowed!

Each hat a character, bold and bright,
With funny twists, they took their flight.
In royal halls of laughter's grace,
The crowned folks danced at a merry pace.

Whispers from the Wardrobe

In a wardrobe tall, whispers abound,
A cap and scarf were soon spellbound.
"What's under there?" a beret inquired,
"Adventure awaits, let's get inspired!"

A coat with pockets full of dreams,
Spoke tales of giggles and wild schemes.
"Let's don our gear and take a chance,
We'll strut our stuff and do a dance!"

The boots did stomp, the shoes did glide,
As every door swung open wide.
With hats a-turning, they pranced around,
In the wardrobe's heart, laughter was found!

"From funky fedoras to silly caps,
Each outfit's got a tale that taps.
So let us spin and twist our fate,
In fashion's laugh, we celebrate!"

Chronicles on the Crown

In a town where hats grow on trees,
A raccoon wore one, oh what a tease!
With a top hat so tall, and one made of cheese,
He danced in the rain, with the greatest of ease.

A penguin joined in with a feathered fedora,
He slipped and he slid, looking quite the explorer.
With a wink and a grin, he claimed the aurora,
While crowding around was a scruffy old quora.

An owl in a beanie wore spectacles round,
Reciting some rhymes to the squirrels on the ground.
With each silly verse, laughter did abound,
As hats of all shapes spun and twirled all around.

Thus stories unwind with these hat-wearing folk,
Whimsical wonders, laughter bespoke.
In every odd hat, a new tale they stoke,
In the chronicles grand, where joy is the cloak.

Whimsical Crowns and Enchanted Tales

In a kingdom where crowns were quite absurd,
A cat wore a flower, his purring deferred.
The kings wore their jester hats, how they stirred,
While giggling at knights, their jokes heard but slurred.

A sandwich with lettuce sat snug on a head,
With pickles like jewels, and crumbs as the spread.
All gathered to hear tales of dreams wildly fed,
As the king did declare, 'Let us dance instead!'

A dragon in sunglasses basked under the sun,
Claiming his crown was made of sweet bun.
With laughter and jokes, the battles were won,
A fest for all creatures: no need for a gun.

So they danced on the hills, in hats of delight,
With flourishes, twirls, under stars glowing bright.
In whimsical crowns, every tale took flight,
As friends laughed together, till late in the night.

The Topper of Dreams

In a world where dreams float atop heads so bright,
A squirrel wore a sombrero, oh what a sight!
Twirling and tumbling, he danced with delight,
While a parrot in clogs gave a musical fright.

A hedgehog in velvet proclaimed he was wise,
With a crown made of marshmallows, to everyone's surprise.
He told all the critters, with glittering eyes,
That a sprinkle of humor would spice up their skies.

An octopus spun plates, with mittens in tow,
While frogs in berets did a spectacular show.
From ribbons to sparkles, in colors that glow,
Every topper a dream, with laughter the flow.

As night fell upon this bright caper parade,
The joy of their antics would never quite fade.
In hats full of dreams, none felt they delayed.
With every kind chuckle, a memory made.

Chapeaux of the Heart

With chapeaux in my dreams, I gallivant wide,
A bunny in bonnets, full of charm and pride.
Spinning tales of delight, where laughter can't hide,
Every silly story, with joy as the guide.

A goldfish with goggles, who tells from the bowl,
In a hat made of shells, oh what a role!
As friends gather round – each a joyous soul,
In chapeaux of the heart, they all take a stroll.

A turtle in glasses shared secrets so sweet,
While a dragon in mittens danced light on his feet.
In hats of all sizes, adventures repeat,
With giggles and fun, their joy was complete.

Thus in hats of their hearts, they'll forever reside,
Where stories are crafted, and laughter's the tide.
With every slight twist, humor will guide,
In chapeaux of the heart, let the fun be our pride.

Threads and Trajectories

In a closet full of hats, quite the sight,
A sailor's cap next to a wizard's delight.
Each one holds a tale, a quirky spin,
Of dragons and darlings, let the fun begin!

The beret sits fancy, with a tilt so bold,
While the baseball cap whispers secrets untold.
From the jester's grin to the crown of a queen,
Every thread weaves a laugh, oh what a scene!

The feathered flapper, all glam and spree,
Dances with a beanie, as carefree as can be.
Funny encounters in the world of headgear,
Each twist of the fabric brings joy and cheer.

So grab a new cap, don't hesitate,
Join in the fun, keep your spirits straight.
With every new style, a chuckle we'll find,
In this hat-tastic world, with laughter entwined!

Twists of the Topper

A cowboy hat strolls with a swagger and sway,
While a top hat exclaims, "I'm formal today!"
The beanie just chuckles, all cozy and warm,
In this hat party chaos, you can't help but charm.

One day a fedora thinks it's quite sly,
Attempts a quick dance with a colorful tie.
Oh, but the sunhat just giggles with glee,
As it keeps on blocking all mischief you see!

The straw hat is boasting of summers so bright,
While the traffic cone cap glows orange in spite.
Each twist of their fabric tells stories anew,
Of hat-wearing heroes, both silly and true.

So tip your strange lid, let the laughter flow,
With all of these toppers, the fun will just grow.
In this wild headwear, with quirks all about,
The joy of the journey, leave no doubt!

Tales from the Tasseled

With tassels a-swaying, the antics unfold,
A hat full of giggles, so brazen, so bold.
A sombrero spins tales of fiestas el cielo,
While a knit cap shares secrets, soft, warm, and mellow.

A pirate's tricorn sits with a mischievous grin,
Plotting adventures on waves that begin.
The wizard's tall hat, with stars all aglow,
Conjures up laughter in a magical show.

The newsboy cap whispers of pigeons and parks,
While the bejeweled beret makes everyone spark.
Each tassel a story, each rim a new jest,
In this world of headwear, we're clearly the best!

So gather your buddies, let's celebrate flair,
With tales from the tasseled, we haven't a care.
In laughter heaped high, we'll tip our fine hats,
And share tales of whimsy; what's cooler than that?

Each Cap a Canvas

From crayons and markers, we'll paint our delight,
Each cap a canvas for fun to ignite.
A skater's cap splashed with colors so bright,
While a beret invites dreams of fancy flight.

The hard hat is ready for games on the street,
With stickers and sketches, it brings funkiness heat.
A ghostly white beanie with eyes all aglow,
Haunting us gently, in winter's white snow.

So let's toss on hats of all shapes divine,
With laughter and art, our imaginations shine.
Each cap tells a story, a giggle or two,
In this whimsical world where each dream comes true.

So gather your brushes, paint laughter and cheer,
In hats filled with stories, we'll spread joy far and near.
As each cap transforms, we share smiles galore,
In this hat-loving wonder, who could ask for more?

Headpieces of Horizon

A tall top hat, looking quite grand,
With rabbits and cards that magically stand.
A feathered beret that wiggles in glee,
Flapping like birds, oh what could it be!

A beanie with beans that giggles at dawn,
Juggling the chores while you're mowing the lawn.
A wizard's cap with sparkles that glow,
Casting some spells on the neighbor's pet crow!

A sailor's hat sailing the seas made of ink,
While a sun hat just sits, sipping lemonade drink.
Each one with a tale, each one brings a laugh,
Frolicking headpieces on their goofy path!

So, grab any hat from the colorful rack,
You'll find a new story with each silly knack.
In this land of headpieces, oh what a delight,
Where laughter and fashion dance day and night!

Layers of Legend

A crown of spaghetti, who knew it could reign?
It twirls in the wind with a glorious mane.
A baseball cap with cosmic design,
Throwing a curveball that's simply divine!

A sombrero so large it blocks out the sun,
It shakes with each beat, just trying to have fun.
A newsboy cap with a mischievous grin,
Whispers to secrets hidden deep within!

A wizard's hat stuck in a blender of fate,
Mixing stories sweet, you're just a tad late.
A party hat filled with confetti and cheer,
Telling wild tales, drawing friends ever near!

So layer your legends, stack 'em up high,
With each little tale, oh my, oh my!
For hats bring together the laughter we harvest,
In the kingdom of stories, they're truly the smartest!

The Fascinator of Fate

A cloche that whispers the gossip of bees,
Crafting small giggles that drift on the breeze.
A fascinator perched like a mischievous sprite,
With ribbons and laughter, it dances in flight!

A helmet adorned with jellybean charms,
Rescue operations with candy for arms.
A sunhat that squints at the clouds in the sky,
Paddling through puddles, oh my, oh my!

A pirate's tricorn that's gone off the rails,
Telling tall tales of shipwrecks and gales.
A crown of daisies, sprouting wild and bold,
Giggling at stories that never grow old!

In every grand hat, there's a tale waiting here,
With laughter and whimsy, let's give a cheer!
For fate wears a fascinator woven with glee,
In every mad moment, there's adventure, you see!

Resplendent Realities

An alien helmet that buzzes and clicks,
Perfect for meetings with space-travel tricks.
A Viking's horned hat, all bristly and proud,
Bellowing laughter, attracting a crowd!

A chapeau adorned with whimsical cheese,
That squeaks out the tales of a mouse's expertise.
A jester's cap riddled with bells that go ring,
Tickling the hearts of all who dare swing!

A news anchor's hat with a camera's bright flash,
Reporting bold stories, delivering with dash.
A floral headband that whispers in bloom,
Telling sweet secrets in every room!

So don your fine headpieces, both silly and grand,
In a realm where each style gives a chuckle at hand.
Resplendent realities await a good jest,
In this carnival of stories, we simply are blessed!

Headgear of Whimsy

A jester's cap with bells that ring,
Worn by the cat who loves to sing.
A sombrero big for a tiny mouse,
Dancing around, having fun in the house.

A chef's hat tall on a pup so spry,
Flipping pancakes, oh me, oh my!
With each funny flip, it spins in the air,
The dog winks at us; it's just a dog's flair.

An explorer's helmet on a goldfish bright,
Swimming through jungles, oh what a sight!
With a wink and a wink, the fish finds its way,
Looking for treasures that sparkle and sway.

A pirate's tricorn on a cow in the barn,
Mooing for treasure, oh, isn't it charm?
Sailing the seas of the haystack's embrace,
Searching for plunder in this grassy place.

Fables in Fabric

A top hat with tales of olden town,
Worn by a turtle who never frowns.
With a monocle gleaming, he spins a good yarn,
Of adventures grand on a field of grass and barn.

A beanie on a bear with cozy intent,
Snug and warm, oh, the time he spent.
Riding a bicycle, oh what a scene,
With a cupcake basket, all sprinkles and cream!

A bonnet of flowers on a goat quite spry,
Leaping for joy, grazing under the sky.
With a giggle and bleat, she hops through the door,
Wearing her blossoms, she's never a bore.

A wizard's hat on a squirrel so small,
Conjuring nuts with a flick of his shawl.
In a magical forest, he casts a sweet spell,
Enchanting the acorns, oh isn't that swell?

The Tale-Teller's Toppers

A crown made of popcorn sits on a raccoon,
Claiming titles of mischief under the moon.
With kernels of laughter, he tells silly tales,
While juggling pinecones and befriending snails.

A fedora tilted on a dog with a grin,
Scratching a vinyl with his paw and a spin.
Playing the tunes that make all things dance,
The neighbors all laugh; who knew dogs could prance?

A beret perched lightly on a clever frog,
Painting the lilies, the pond is his blog.
With strokes of humor and swirls of delight,
His art comes alive in the shimmering night.

A party hat worn by a frog on a log,
Throwing a bash for each snail and each dog.
With a squeak and a bop, the fun never ends,
As confetti of daisies cascades on his friends.

Chapeaus of Change

A baseball cap rests on a wise old owl,
Coaching young critters with an assertive growl.
Teaching them strategies, how to take flight,
Underneath the stars in the soft glowing night.

A wedding veil on a chipmunk so spry,
Practicing dance moves, oh me, oh my!
With a twirl and a spin, he takes to the floor,
As the other chipmunks cheer and adore.

A bearded cap on a shifty sly fox,
Stealing the spotlight from the family of hawks.
With a smile and a wink, he snatches the scene,
Flipping the script in this comedy glean.

A sun hat on a tortoise, slow moving but bright,
Sipping on lemonade, oh, what a sight!
He tells all his buddies to take life real slow,
With hats of all stories, together they grow.

The Cap that Thought

There once was a cap, oh so spry,
It pondered its purpose, oh my,
"Am I for a hero, or just for a laugh?"
It rolled on a wiggle, delight in its path.

With a flip and a flop, it bounced down the street,
It met a tall top hat, both felt quite the feat,
"Why so stiff?" asked the cap, with a very wide grin,
"I'm dignified, dear friend, I shall always win!"

They laughed and they chirped in the bright afternoon,
A trio formed close, under the lazy sun's tune,
A beanie pitched in, with a mischievous style,
Together they juggled, in pure, silly guile.

So if you've a cap that makes you giggle,
Wear it boldly, give life a wiggle,
For every good laugh, there's a tale just begun,
With hats in the air, let the stories be spun!

Toppers of Tales

In a land where the toppers are truly bizarre,
Lived a fez that dreamed it could dance at the bar,
With a hop and a twirl, it stole every scene,
While the bowler just sighed, less festive, less keen.

A sombrero joined in, with a colorful sway,
"Let's party!" it cheered, in a big, bold display,
"But what about reason?" the beret did fret,
"Life's too short for rules," the top hat then said.

So they partied and pranced, in the moon's soft embrace,
The crown sang a ballad, with elegance and grace,
While the caps on the sidelines joined in with a cheer,
For a night with no worries, was finally here!

And as dawn started breaking, they swayed home in glee,
Each topper a story, each giggle a spree,
In a world full of toppers, great tales did ignite,
For hats full of laughter can soar with delight!

Whimsical Crowns

Oh the crowns in the kingdom had quite the delight,
They each had a tale shining oh so bright,
A jester's bright cap, with bells jingling near,
Would prank every royal, then disappear!

A tiara did glimmer, with jewels so grand,
Claiming, "I'm royal, I rule this fine land!"
But the knit cap with humor thought, "That's just fluff,
True regality comes from being just tough!"

They launched into banter, with hats full of flair,
And decided to party without any care,
With a dance and a twirl, they all joined as one,
In a fiesta of laughter, the real crown was fun!

So whenever you see a crown sparkling bright,
Remember the tales that ignited that night,
For whimsy and chuckles are what truly astound,
In a realm where each cap wears its joy all around!

Hued Dreams Above

With colors aflow, the hats spun with grace,
A polka dot cap had an adventurous pace,
"I'll travel the world on a whim and a dare!"
While the fedora just chuckled, without all the flair.

A beanie declared, "I'm cozy yet bold!"
"But silly is better," the eye patch cap told,
"For laughter can echo in every bright hue,
And with fun on our heads, there's much we can do!"

So they made a parade, with each story they shared,
The crowds gathered 'round, oh how they all dared,
In a whirlwind of colors, the hats danced all day,
A festival of giggles, what a splendid display!

When nightfall arrived, and the stars lit the sky,
The crowns gathered close, each hat gave a sigh,
For in dreams that they wore, the spirit would thrive,
In hues full of laughter, they'd always survive!

Every Brim Tells a Tale

Underneath a wide-brimmed hat,
A cat once wore a pair of spats.
It danced around with such delight,
While sipping tea, it felt just right.

A fedora held a secret flair,
With pocket squirrels and a mischievous air.
They planned a heist with nuts galore,
But tripped and spilled on the dance floor.

A beanie told of winter's chill,
Of snowball fights and endless thrill.
Its woolly warmth wrapped around,
As laughter echoed all around.

In every hat, a story spun,
Of offbeat humor and silly fun.
So wear your hat with a grin so wide,
And let the tales flow like a joyous tide.

Fantasies in Fabrics

A polka-dot cap on a dreaming head,
Whispered tales of buttered bread.
It promised a world of sweets so bright,
Where jellybeans lit up the night.

A patchwork hat, all colors combined,
Held secrets of a very strange kind.
It laughed at socks lost in the wash,
And skated on rainbows, oh what a posh!

A sunhat wide with floral prints,
Swung over to join the funny hints.
It basked in rays and soaked in cheer,
Inviting ants for a picnic here.

With every thread a story weaves,
Of whimsy caught in playful leaves.
Dare to dream what each could share,
In fabrics spun with laughter rare.

The Meeting of Minds and Millinery

Two hats met on a sunny day,
A sombrero asked, "What do you say?"
The beret chuckled, puffs of romance,
"Let's start a dance, let's take a chance!"

They swirled and twirled, with flair and grace,
A top hat joined, trying to keep pace.
"I'm here for the charm and no doubt the fun,
Let's crown this party, we're never done!"

Bowler hats chimed in with a 'cheerio',
Wearing little bows and a flowered glow.
"Let's share our tales, spun with delight,
Of roles we've played in day and night!"

So hats from all over began to chat,
From crazy topknots to a dapper flat.
A committee of fun, with styles so bold,
Where laughter was plenty, and hearts turned gold.

Echoes of Eccentricity

A green fez perched on a walrus's snout,
Said, "Life's too short, let's dance about!"
It juggled fish while the crowd all cheered,
Such quirky antics, they never feared.

On a rainy day, a cap made of cheese,
Called out, "Come join, let's make it a spree!"
Umbrellas laughed as puddles splashed,
In a spectacle where time just dashed.

A crumpled cap with a sneaker-like flair,
Sang silly songs, causing quite the scare.
With every riff and melody sweet,
It had the whole party dancing on feet.

With each odd hat, a giggle arises,
In the realm where fun never disguises.
So gather round, let laughter reign,
In echoes of weirdness, we'll never wane.

The Cap Collector's Diary

In a closet stacked with caps so bright,
Each one whispers secrets, day and night.
There's a floppy sunhat, wide as a kite,
Claiming it's cooler than a winter's bite.

A baseball cap from a distant game,
Swears it caught the winning frame.
A beanie claims it's full of fame,
Yet in a snowstorm, it felt the shame.

The cowboy hat likes to strut and sway,
Saying it's the best for a rodeo day.
But it just collects dust, I dare say,
Dreaming of horses that never play.

Oh, the antics of these caps on my shelf,
Each one a character, a comic elf.
I laugh at their tales, like a storybook self,
In this cap-collecting, whimsical wealth!

Hats: Windows to the Soul

A top hat's elegant, a true delight,
But wobbles like jelly when held too tight.
A fedora claims it's the true knight,
Yet trips on its brim, what a silly sight!

A beret winks with a cheeky grin,
Saying it's fancy, let the fun begin.
It dances on heads like it just can't win,
While the poor sunhat feels the heat from within.

The straw hat giggles, sips tea with grace,
Boasting of summers and sunlit space.
But gets blown away in a silly chase,
Leaving behind just a smile in its place.

Each hat's a story, yet so absurd,
With feathers and frills, their tales are stirred.
In the grand parade of headgear blurred,
Life's a circus, and we're all deferred!

Embroidered Secrets Beneath

Underneath layers, in a grand display,
Lies a cap that's had quite the wild day.
With threads of laughter, it weaves its way,
Spinning whispers of mischief at play.

A beaded design, so intricate and neat,
Claims it was worn on a giant's feet.
But really it traveled to a funky street,
Where retro dances made life a treat.

The sunhat's brim hides a ticklish tale,
Of a chase with a bird that forgot to sail.
While the poncho hat tells of a windy gale,
Leaving its owner to flail and rail.

In stitches and seams, secrets confide,
Each cap a world where humor won't hide.
Beneath those bright weaves, joy takes pride,
In a closet of wonders where giggles abide!

Fables in Fabric

A wizard's cap with a twist of fate,
Claims it can conjure up magic so great.
But all it does is cause folks to wait,
For the laundry to finish—it's really quite late!

The pirate hat, oh, what a tale,
Boasts of treasures found in a shady trail.
Yet today, it's guarding a missing mail,
With birds that tease and a dog that wails.

A chef's hat fluffs with pride so tall,
Singing of soufflés that never fall.
But in the kitchen, it's just a small stall,
For burnt toast is all that it can recall.

Each fabric holds laughter, stitched with delight,
In adventures and mischief that take to flight.
With every pop hat and whimsical sight,
These fables in fabric make every day bright!

Fables Encapsulated

In the forest, a squirrel wore a cat,
He scurried about, thinking he's quite fat.
A wise old owl just gave a chuckle,
While the rabbit danced in a jazzy shuffle.

A turtle donned a wizard's cap bright,
Casting spells that just made things light.
A frog tried a crown, but it slipped off his head,
As he croaked in laughter, not quite misled.

The fox wore a bonnet, frills, and lace,
Pretending to be an elegant grace.
But with a quick dip in the mud he got,
He found fancy headwear isn't all that hot.

So remember each tale of creatures in hats,
Their silly adventures, and sparkly chats.
In this whimsical land of quirky attire,
Every headpiece leads to laughter we admire.

Toppers of the Transformative

A chef had a sombrero, big and round,
He stirred the soup with flair and sound.
The spices danced like a mariachi band,
As he twirled on the stove, much to the fans.

An astronaut sported a pirate's eye-patch,
Claiming the moon was his rare catch.
"Arr matey!" he shouted as he floated so high,
While stars giggled quietly in the sky.

A penguin in shades slid down on his belly,
Rolling in style, oh so very silly.
He'd quip about freezing with every slide,
With fashion like that, he'd never hide!

So stack on those toppers, both silly and bold,
Transforming tales into laughter to unfold.
These whimsical wears make the world seem bright,
And in every adventure, there's shared delight.

The Headpiece Chronicles

In a kingdom where chickens ruled the day,
A prince wore a tiara more frilly than gay.
He clucked and he strutted with pompous flair,
While peasants snickered at the crown in his hair.

A knight in a helmet that shimmered with pearls,
Rushed off to battle amid giggling curls.
"Fear not the fire!" he boldly proclaimed,
But tripped in the moat and the laughter was aimed.

Through valleys of flowers, a jester ran free,
Bouncing on rooftops, quite droll as can be.
His hat had bells that jingled with glee,
As he shouted, "My friends, come dance with me!"

Each hat tells a tale of a character proud,
Creating a chorus, both silly and loud.
So don't shy from the quirky and strange,
For every fine headpiece brings joy and exchange.

Plumes of Possibility

A dapper old owl wore a feathered plume,
While singing to the moon, lighting up the gloom.
His monotone voice brought giggles from all,
As squirrels and rabbits rushed to the call.

A bunny with goggles pretended to fly,
In a hat full of eggs, he aimed for the sky.
He burrowed through daisies, hopping so high,
Proclaiming, "This launch, oh my, is just spry!"

A bear with a fedora sipped honey in style,
While bees buzzed around him, a whimsical trial.
"Don't mind me, folks, I'm just here for a feast,"
As he started to dance, a true honey beast.

So gather your plumes, both silly and sweet,
For every hat worn brings life to our feet.
With laughter and whimsy, let stories ignite,
Each headpiece unravels a world full of light.